JULIE SOUCAIL

# HOW TO COOK

# FRE

# PASTRY

*50 traditional French recipes*



MADE IN FRANCE

ISBN: 979-1-03010-190-4
Legal deposit: March 2017
Printed in Slovenia

Tana éditions, a department of Édi8
12, avenue d'Italie
75013 Paris
Tel.: 01 44 16 09 00
Fax: 01 44 16 09 01
www.tana.fr

JULIE SOUCAIL

# HOW TO COOK FRENCH PASTRY

## 50 traditional French recipes

PHOTOGRAPHER
FABRICE VEIGAS

MADE IN FRANCE

Tana
éditions

# CONTENTS

# Techniques

Serves **4** to **6** / Preparation: **15** min / Resting: **1** h

# SHORTCRUST *pastry*

- 250 g/2 cups flour
- 1 pinch of salt
- 125 g/½ cup butter at room temperature, cut into small pieces
- 1 egg
- 1 tbsp. water

(opposite pictures)

***1*** Mix the flour and salt. Make a well and place the butter in the centre. Mix gently to coat the pieces of butter and then rub the mixture with your fingertips. Add the egg and water, kneading briefly until the dough is smooth. Form a ball and let it rest for a minimum of 1 hour in the refrigerator. Remove the dough from the refrigerator 15 to 20 minutes before rolling out.

Serves **4** to **6** / Preparation: **10** min / Resting: **1** h

# SWEET *pastry*

- 250 g/2 cups flour
- 50 g/¼ cup sugar
- 1 pinch of salt
- 125 g/½ cup cold butter, cut into small pieces
- 1 egg
- 1 tbsp. milk

***1*** Place the flour, sugar and salt in a bowl, add the butter, rubbing the mixture with your fingertips.

***2*** Add the whole egg and the milk. Mix quickly with your fingertips, until the dough is smooth. Form the dough into a ball and let it rest for a minimum of 1 hour in the refrigerator. Remove the dough from the refrigerator 10 to 15 minutes before rolling out.

For about **20** choux / Preparation: **20** min / Resting: **5** min / Cooking: **20** to **25** min

# CHOUX *pastry*

- 75 g/⅓ cup butter
- 15 cl/⅝ cup milk
- 7 g/½ tbsp. caster sugar
- 150 g/1 ¼ cups flour
- 4 eggs
- 3 g/ ½ tsp. salt

***1*** Cut the butter into pieces. Pour the milk into a saucepan, add the sugar, salt and butter. Melt on high heat. When the mixture begins to boil, add the flour all at once, mixing vigorously with a wooden spoon. Keep stirring over a medium heat until the mixture forms a ball and detaches from the edges of the pan.

***2*** Remove the pan from the heat and leave to stand for 5 minutes.

***3*** Add the whole eggs one after the other, mixing each time until the egg is completely incorporated into the dough. The mixture should be smooth and shiny.

***4*** Preheat the oven to 400°F.

***5*** Form the choux, preferably using a piping bag with a nozzle, on a baking sheet covered with baking paper. Bake for 20 to 25 minutes according to the recipe (profiteroles, eclairs, chouquettes) without opening the oven door during cooking. Slip a small bowl of water into the oven for a softer choux.

Preparation: **30** min / Resting: **14** h **20**

# PUFF PASTRY

## *unleavened* (*for tarts and king cake*)

- 250 g/2 cups butter
- 250 g/2 cups flour
  + a little for the worktop
- 12.5 cl/½ cup ice water
- 1 pinch of salt

***1*** The night before, cut the butter into small cubes and place it in the freezer, making sure that the pieces aren't touching (spread them on a sheet of baking paper or aluminium foil).

***2*** The next day, place all the ingredients in a mixer bowl. Mix on maximum power for 15 to 30 seconds. You should get a coarse, sandy mixture. Flour the worktop, pour the contents of the mixer bowl onto the worktop (if your mixer bowl is not very large, proceed in 2 steps with half of the ingredients). Knead quickly until you can form a ball.

***3*** Flour a rolling pin, and if necessary flour the worktop again. Spread the dough as thinly as possible, giving it the shape of a rectangle. Turn the dough regularly and flour the worktop and rolling pin so that it does not stick.

***4*** Form a roll by gradually folding the wide part of the rectangle over on itself, pressing with the palm of your hand after each turn. Pass the rolling pin over it to flatten it gently and then roll it around itself, tightening, to form a snail. Wrap in cling film and refrigerate for 30 minutes.

***5*** Take the dough out of the refrigerator. Set it down so that the layers are facing you and not on top.

***6*** Flatten the dough roughly to form a block, maintaining the edges so that the layers remain inside. Gently roll out the block lengthways with the rolling pin, then fold in 3.

***7*** Roll out the dough according to the preparation of your choice. Refrigerate for 20 minutes before use.

Serves **4** to **6** / Preparation: **30** min / Resting: **14** h **30**

# PUFF PASTRY *leavened* (for viennoiserie)

- 250 g/2 cups butter
- 12 g/1 heaped tbsp. fresh baker's yeast (alternatively dry yeast)
- 250 g/2 cups flour
- 10 cl/½ cup ice water
- 25 g/2 tbsp. sugar + 1 pinch
- 1 pinch of salt

***1*** The night before, cut the butter into small cubes and place it in the freezer, making sure that the pieces aren't touching (spread them on a sheet of baking paper or aluminium foil).

***2*** Dissolve the yeast in 3 cl warm water with a pinch of sugar. Leave to stand until small bubbles form on the surface.

***3*** Pour the flour, sugar and yeast into a mixer bowl and mix quickly. Add the frozen butter, salt and ice water. Then proceed as in the recipe on p. 12.

SUGAR
ZUCKER
SUCRE
500 ml
400 ml
300 ml
200 ml
100 ml
1 PINT
3/4 PINT
1/2 PINT
1/4 PINT

# Recipes

Serves **1** / Preparation: **20** min / Resting: **1** h / Cooking: **25** min

# CRÈME caramel

- 75 g/⅓ cup sugar
- 1 egg
- 10 cl/⅖ cup milk
- 5 cl/⅕ cup single cream
- ½ tsp. natural vanilla extract

***1*** Pour 30 g/2 tbsp. sugar into a small saucepan, add 1 tsp. water. Gently rotate the pan so that the sugar is completely soaked. Cook over a medium heat until the mixture forms an amber coloured caramel. Immediately place the caramel into the bottom of a ramekin.

***2*** Whisk the egg with the remaining sugar until the mixture turns white.

***3*** Pour the milk and cream into a saucepan, add the vanilla extract. Stir and bring to the boil. Pour the boiling mixture over the beaten egg, whisking until the mixture is smooth. Filter through a fine sieve and pour into the ramekin, on top of the caramel.

***4*** Preheat the oven to 350°F. Place the ramekin in a baking dish. Add boiling water up to two thirds of the height of the ramekin. Bake for about 25 minutes until the custard is set.

***5*** Remove the ramekin from the oven, let it cool in the bain marie. Chill for at least 1 hour.

***6*** Gently slide a knife around the cream and turn out upside-down onto a plate.

Serves **6** / Preparation: **10** min / Cooking: **1** h **5**

# CARAMEL rice pudding

- 250 g/1¼ cups caster sugar
- 90 cl/3¾ cups milk
- 1 large vanilla pod
- 180 g/1 cup pudding rice

***1*** Preheat the oven to 350°F.

***2*** Prepare the caramel: put 200 g/1 cup sugar in a saucepan, add 7 cl/⅓ cup water and place over a medium heat, stirring gently from time to time until the caramel turns a nice amber colour. Transfer to a heavy-bottomed pan or cooking pot.

***3*** Put the milk and remaining sugar in a saucepan. Open the vanilla pod and extract the seeds, add the seeds and pod to the contents of the pan. Bring to the boil, then sprinkle in the rice. Mix and bring back to the boil, then cook over a low heat for 10 minutes, stirring frequently.

***4*** Remove the vanilla pod and transfer the rice pudding to the pan, on top of the caramel. Bake for 50 minutes.

***5*** During cooking, stir 2 or 3 times to incorporate the skin that forms on the surface of the mixture.

***6*** Serve warm or cold.

Serves **6** / Preparation: **30** min / Resting: **5** h **15** / Cooking: **12** min

# CHESTNUT *mousse*

- 3 sheets of gelatine
- 20 cl/⅞ cup milk
- 1 tsp. liquid vanilla extract
- 3 egg yolks
- 30 g/2 tbsp. caster sugar
- 250 g/1 cup sweet chestnut puree
- 20 cl/⅞ cup whipping cream
- Sponge finger biscuits to serve (optional)

***1*** Soak the gelatine sheets in a bowl of cold water.

***2*** Pour the milk and vanilla extract into a saucepan, stir and bring to the boil.

***3*** Whisk the egg yolks with the sugar until the mixture whitens. Pour the warm milk gradually over the mixture whilst whisking.

***4*** Transfer the mixture into the saucepan, stir constantly over a medium/low heat for 10 to 12 minutes until the cream thickens (be careful not to cook it too long or the mixture will become lumpy).

***5*** Remove the pan from the heat. Wring the leaves of gelatine by pressing them tightly in your hand, stir them into the hot cream together with the chestnut purée.

***6*** Pour the cream into a bowl (preferably metal). Place the bowl and the blades of the whisk in the freezer for 15 minutes.

***7*** Whip the cream with an electric whisk until firm.

***8*** Fold the chestnut cream little by little into the whipped cream, lifting delicately with a spatula.

***9*** Divide the mousse into 6 cups and set aside for 5 hours.

***10*** Serve with sponge finger biscuits.

Serves **4** / Preparation: **20** min / Resting: **2** h minimum / Cooking: **5** min

# CHOCOLATE *mousse*

- 200 g/7 oz. dark chocolate, minimum 70% cocoa
- 50 g/¼ cup unsalted butter, soft
- 4 eggs
- 1 tbsp. rum or Grand Marnier® (optional)
- 50 g/¼ cup caster sugar
- Cocoa powder for decoration

***1*** Melt the chocolate in a bain-marie* or microwave oven. Cut the butter into small pieces and incorporate it into the melted chocolate, stirring to obtain a smooth cream.
***2*** Break the eggs, separating the whites from the yolks. Add the yolks one by one to the previous mixture, stirring well each time. Then add the rum or Grand Marnier®.
***3*** Whisk the whites into peaks with an electric whisk. When they start to firm up, gradually add the sugar. Keep whisking until the whites are firm. Quickly incorporate 1 large spoonful of egg whites into the chocolate mixture. When it turns smooth and creamy, gradually fold in the rest of the egg whites, gently lifting with a spatula to obtain a foamy, airy texture.
***4*** Cover the mousse with film and chill for at least 2 hours before serving. Divide the mousse into individual bowls, and decorate with cocoa powder sprinkled through a fine sieve.

* Method for melting chocolate in a bain-marie: you will need a saucepan and a narrower container that fits in the saucepan. Break the chocolate into pieces and place in the container. Pour water into the saucepan, making sure that the level does not rise above the edge of the container. Heat the water until it simmers, then place the container into the saucepan. Heat gently, stirring occasionally until the chocolate is melted.

* Method for melting chocolate in a microwave oven: break the chocolate, place it in a non-metallic container, heat on medium power (approximately 300 watts) for 30 second intervals, mixing well each time, until the chocolate is fully melted.

Everyone has their own recipe and there are hundreds of possibilities using different chocolate flavours. The most important thing is to indulge yourself.

Serves **4** / Preparation: **20** min / Cooking: **15** min

# ORANGE *sabayon*

- 3 oranges
- 4 egg yolks
- 80 g/3/8 cup caster sugar
- 1 pinch of salt
- 15 cl/5/8 cup strained orange juice
- 1 tbsp. Grand Marnier® or Cointreau®
- 1 knob of butter for ramekins

***1*** Peel the oranges, gently pass the blade of a knife between the membranes to separate the segments. Let them drain through a strainer or on kitchen paper and then distribute them between 4 pre-buttered ramekins.

***2*** Whisk the egg yolks with the sugar and salt until the mixture whitens and then add the orange juice.

***3*** Prepare a bain-marie and whip the cream constantly until it thickens, becomes foamy and triples in volume. Remove from the heat and add the Grand Marnier® or Cointreau®.

***4*** Divide the cream between the ramekins, on top of the orange segments.

***5*** Place the sabayons under the grill for a few minutes until the cream is golden brown.

The sabayon is of Italian origin and dates from the sixteenth century. To give it a more Italian flavour, you can replace the Grand Marnier® or Cointreau® with marsala.

Serves **6** / Preparation: **25** min / Freezing: **15** min / Resting: **15** min / Cooking: **40** min

# VANILLA BAVARIAN cream

- 25 cl/1 cup whipping cream
- 6 sheets of gelatine
- 50 cl/2 cups whole milk
- 1 vanilla pod
- 5 egg yolks
- 180 g/1 cup caster sugar

For the coulis:
- 500 g/17 oz. strawberries
- 200 g/2 cups icing sugar
- 2 tbsp. lemon juice

***1*** Pour the cream into a bowl. Place the bowl and the blades of the whisk in the freezer for 15 minutes.
***2*** Soak the gelatine leaves in cold water.
***3*** Pour the milk into a saucepan, remove the seeds from the vanilla pod, add them to the milk followed by the pod. Bring to the boil.
***4*** Whip the egg yolks with the sugar until the mixture whitens. Remove the vanilla pod and pour the hot milk over the mixture while whipping.
***5*** Transfer the mixture back to the saucepan and thicken over a low heat, stirring until the cream coats the spoon.
***6*** Wring the gelatine sheets in your hand to remove the water. Off the heat, add them to the hot cream, stirring well. Filter through a fine sieve.
***7*** Whip the cream and add to the mixture.
***8*** Butter a savarin mould or cake tin and pour in the mixture. Refrigerate for 12 hours until set.
***9*** Prepare the coulis: wash and dry the strawberries and remove their stalks. Mix them carefully with the icing sugar and lemon juice. Filter the coulis through a fine sieve.
***10*** Serve the Bavarian cream topped with the strawberry coulis.

Serves **4** / Preparation: **15** min / Cooking: **18** min / Refrigeration: **2** h

# CRÈME *brûlée*

- 2 eggs + 2 yolks
- 45 g/¼ cup caster sugar
- 25 cl/1 cup cream
- 6 cl/¼ cup milk
- 1 tsp. liquid vanilla extract
- 4 tbsp. brown sugar

***1*** Preheat the oven to 200°F.

***2*** Whip the whole eggs and yolks with the caster sugar until the mixture doubles in volume.

***3*** Pour the cream, milk and vanilla extract into a saucepan, mix and heat until it begins to simmer. Using a ladle, gradually and gently fold the hot cream into the sugar and egg mixture.

***4*** Divide the cream into 4 ramekins. Arrange the creams in a large dish, gently pour boiling water into the dish until it reaches halfway up the ramekins. Bake for 20 to 25 minutes, the creams are cooked when they are firm at the edge and still a little wobbly in the centre.

***5*** Allow to cool and then refrigerate for at least 2 hours.

***6*** When serving, lightly and evenly sprinkle the surface of the creams with brown sugar. Caramelize with a chef's blowtorch or pass quickly under the grill.

***7*** Leave to cool for a few minutes before serving to let the caramel harden.

The caramelization of brown sugar is what adds the crunch to this classic French dessert.

Serves **6** / Preparation: **30** min / Cooking: **25** min / Refrigeration: **2** h

# FLOATING islands

- 4 eggs
- 50 cl/2 cups milk
- 200 g/1 cup caster sugar
- 2 tsp. liquid vanilla extract

**1** Break the eggs, separating the white from the yolks.
**2** Pour the milk and vanilla extract into a saucepan, mix and bring to a boil.
**3** Whip the egg yolks with 50 g sugar until the mixture whitens. Pour the warm milk gradually over the mixture whilst whipping. Pour the mixture into the saucepan and place on a medium-low heat for 10 to 12 minutes. Stir constantly until the cream thickens (be careful not to cook it for too long, or it will become lumpy).
**4** Pour the cream into a bowl, leave to cool and then cover with cling film and refrigerate for 2 hours.
**5** Preheat the oven to 250°F.
**6** Whisk the egg whites into firm peaks. When they begin to stiffen, add 50 g sugar little by little.
**7** Line a baking sheet with baking paper. Make quenelles of beaten egg white using 2 tablespoons and arrange them on the plate. Bake for 5 minutes, then open the oven door and continue cooking for 3 min.
**8** Divide the cream between 6 dishes, place the floating islands on the cream.
**9** Prepare the caramel: Place a sheet of baking paper on a plate. Pour the remaining sugar into a heavy-bottomed saucepan. Add a drop of water, just enough to moisten the sugar. Place over medium-high heat until the sugar melts and turns a nice amber colour. Drizzle the hot caramel onto the baking paper, let it harden and then decorate the floating islands.

Serves **4** / Preparation: **20** min / Cooking: **40** min

# PEAR
# Belle-Hélène

- 4 small, ripe, firm pears
- Juice of ½ lemon
- 80 g/⅜ cup caster sugar
- 80 cl/3⅓ cups water
- 2 tbsp. sliced almonds
- 100 g/3 ½ oz. dark chocolate, 70% cocoa
- 20 g/1 ½ tbsp. butter

***1*** Peel the pears, keeping their stalks intact, and sprinkle with lemon juice.

***2*** Pour the sugar and water into a saucepan and bring to the boil, stirring occasionally to obtain a syrup.

***3*** Lower the flame to a minimum and place the pears into the syrup. Leave to cook for about 25 minutes until tender.

***4*** Remove the pears from the pan with a slotted spoon and place them on serving plates. Let them cool completely.

***5*** Take 25 cl syrup and reduce to one third.

***6*** Brown the sliced almonds in a frying pan without fat.

***7*** Chop the chocolate, melt it on low heat in the reduced syrup, stirring gently. Add the butter cut into small pieces.

***8*** Pour the chocolate sauce over the pears, sprinkle with sliced almonds.

***9*** Serve immediately.

Pear Belle-Hélène was created by Georges-Auguste Escoffier in 1864. The year that Offenbach's opera "La Belle-Hélène" was a hit at the Théâtre des Variétés.

Serves **4** to **6** / Preparation: **20** min / Resting: approx. **1** h **30** / Cooking: **35** min

# BRIOCHE

- 110 g/½ cup butter + 1 knob for the pan
- 10 g/1 level tbsp. fresh yeast
- 5 cl/⅕ cup warm milk
- 250 g/2 cups flour
- 1 tsp. salt
- 30 g/2 tbsp. sugar
- 2 medium eggs+1 yolk

***1*** Remove the butter from the fridge, cut into small pieces and leave at room temperature.

***2*** Dissolve the yeast in the warm milk. Pour the flour into a deep bowl (or better still, a dough mixer), make a well in the middle and add the salt, sugar, dissolved yeast and eggs. Knead the mixture for about ten minutes until the dough is smooth and not sticky (add a little flour if necessary). Add butter and knead quickly to mix it in without melting. Make the dough into a ball and place in a bowl, cover the bowl with cling film to prevent a crust forming and leave to stand for 1 hour in a warm place.

***3*** Grease a cake tin or loaf tin. When the dough has doubled in size, knead quickly again and place into the tin. Let the dough rise, covered with cling film, until it has again doubled in size.

***4*** Preheat the oven to 350°F. Beat the egg yolk with 2 tsp. water and glaze the top of the brioche. Bake for around 35 minutes until golden.

***5*** Turn out the brioche when cooled, but still warm.

Serves **4** to **6** / Preparation: **15** min / Cooking: **45** min

# SPICE *bread*

- 125 g/½ cup butter+1 knob for the pan
- 100 g/⅓ cup honey
- 15 cl/⅝ cup milk
- 200 g/1⅔ cups flour
- 1 pinch salt
- 2 tsp. baking powder
- 50 g/¼ cup brown sugar
- 8 g/1 tsp. pain d'épice spice mix (a blend of aniseed, cloves, nutmeg, cinnamon)
- 1 egg

***1*** Preheat the oven to 350°F.

***2*** Grease a cake tin with butter.

***3*** Heat the honey, milk and butter. Stir.

***4*** Mix the flour, salt, baking powder, brown sugar and spices in a bowl. Gradually add the honey/milk/butter mixture, whisking gently. Work the mixture well until smooth and even. Add the egg, beaten.

***5*** Pour the mixture into the tin and bake for 40-45 minutes.

***6*** Turn out the spice bread and leave to cool on a rack.

Evokes winter, evenings by the fireside and Christmas parties. Makes a delicious snack with tea or, if you really want to indulge, a hot chocolate.

Serves **6** / Preparation: **25** min / Resting: **1** h / Cooking: **40** min

# CRÊPES *Suzette*

- 1 orange (untreated)
- 20 cl/$\frac{7}{8}$ cup of water
- 30 cl/1$\frac{1}{4}$ cup milk
- 2 eggs
- 30 g/2 tbsp. sugar
- 1 generous pinch salt
- 200 g/1$\frac{2}{3}$ cups flour
- 50 g/$\frac{1}{4}$ cup cooled melted butter
- 1 tbsp. sunflower oil

For the sauce
- 90 g/$\frac{2}{5}$ cup butter
- 90 g/$\frac{1}{2}$ cup sugar
- The juice of 3 oranges
- 20 cl/$\frac{7}{8}$ cup Grand Marnier®

***1*** Zest the orange and squeeze. Mix the milk with the water. Beat the eggs together with the salt and sugar. Stir in one third of the milk and water mixture. Add the flour in batches, whisking vigorously to avoid lumps. Pour in the melted butter, stir, then add the remaining milk and water mixture followed by the orange juice and zest. Cover with a cloth and leave to stand for 1 hour at room temperature.

***2*** Grease the pan with a piece of kitchen towel soaked in oil, heat until the pan is nice and hot. Beat the batter and pour one ladleful into the pan. After 1 minute, flip the pancake and cook the other side for around 30 seconds. Transfer to a plate, fold the crepe into a triangle. Repeat with the remaining batter, greasing the pan between each pancake.

***3*** Melt the butter with the sugar in a saucepan, add the orange juice, let the mixture reduce for 2 to 3 minutes. Pour a little sauce into a frying pan, enough to generously cover the bottom, place 4 crepes into the pan and let them warm up, on a medium heat, basting them with the sauce. Pour in 5 cl/$\frac{1}{5}$ cup Grand Marnier®, and flambé. When the flame goes out, transfer the pancakes to a warm plate, top them with the remaining sauce from the pan, and cover to keep them nice and warm. Repeat with the remaining crepes and sauce. Serve hot.

For **10** croissants / Preparation: **25** min / Resting: **1** h **10** / Cooking: **25** min

# CROISSANTS

- 1 puff pastry, leavened (see p. 14)
- 1 egg yolk
- Flour

***1*** Preheat the oven to 410°F.

***2*** Take the dough out of the refrigerator and first flatten it with the palm of your hand. Flour the worktop and roll out the dough with a rolling pin to make a rectangle 4 mm thick.

***3*** Cut out 5 rectangles 12 cm x 12 cm. Make a small triangular notch about 0.5 cm from the base of the triangles and then roll out each triangle from the base towards the point. Give them a crescent shape.

***4*** Arrange the croissants on a lined baking sheet, point down, and let them rest at room temperature for 1 hour.

***5*** Beat the egg yolk and apply it to the croissants with a pastry brush, avoiding the cut edges (this will prevent the lamination from developing completely). Leave to stand for 10 minutes and repeat the procedure.

***6*** Bake at 410°F, point facing upwards, then lower the temperature to 350°F and cook for 25 minutes.

***7*** Remove the croissants from the oven, let them cool on a rack, enjoy while still warm or when completely cooled.

A must for
a French breakfast!

For **8** pains au chocolat / Preparation: **25** min / Resting: **1** h **10** / Cooking: **25** min

# PAINS *au chocolat*

- 1 puff pastry, leavened (see p. 10)
- Flour
- 1 egg yolk
- 12 bars of cooking chocolate for pain au chocolat

What could be more delicious than a small chocolate bar surrounded by puff pastry! Every child's favourite snack!

***1*** Preheat the oven to 410°F.
***2*** Take the dough out of the refrigerator and first flatten it with the palm of your hand. Flour the worktop and roll out the dough with a rolling pin to make a rectangle 4 mm thick. Cut the rolled dough into rectangles 8 cm x 15 cm.
***3*** Lay the wide part of the rectangles facing you. Place a chocolate bar 0.5 cm from the edge and fold the rectangles up to half way, place a second bar of chocolate and roll to the end.
***4*** Arrange the pains au chocolat on a baking sheet covered with baking paper, positioning the join face down and leave to stand for 1 hour.
***5*** Beat the egg yolk and apply it to the breads with a pastry brush. Leave to rest for 10 minutes and repeat the process.
***6*** Bake at 410°F (leave the pains au chocolat on the baking sheet with the join face down) then lower the temperature to 350°F and cook for 25 minutes.
***7*** Remove the pains au chocolat from the oven and let them cool on a rack.

If you cannot get special chocolate bars, you can make them yourself: Melt 150 g chocolate in a bain-marie. Let it cool until it is compact but still malleable. Place it in a piping bag and then make 8 cm long strips on a sheet of baking paper. Let them cool completely before using them.

For **8** turnovers / Preparation: **40** min / Resting: **1** h **10** / Cooking: **55** min

# APPLE turnovers

- 500 g/1 lb apples
- 80 g/⅜ cup sugar
- 1 puff pastry, leavened (see p. 14)
- Flour
- 2 tbsp. milk
- 2 egg yolks

***1*** Peel the apples and cut into cubes. Put them in a saucepan with 50 g sugar and 5 cl water. Cover and cook for 20 to 25 minutes until the apples are tender. Stir.

***2*** Remove the puff pastry from the refrigerator. Flour the rolling pin and worktop and roll out the pastry to a thickness of 3 mm. Using a cookie cutter, cut circles 12 cm in diameter. Roll them out gently with the rolling pin.

***3*** Place the apple mixture in the bottom of the circle, brush a little milk on the edges then close the turnover by folding the upper part over the filling. Press down the edges so that the turnover is tightly closed. Repeat with the rest of the ingredients. Leave to stand for 1 hour.

***4*** Preheat the oven to 410°F.

***5*** Beat the egg yolks and then brush the surface of the turnovers. Refrigerate for 10 minutes. Brush again and then score with the tip of a knife. Bake for 20 to 25 minutes until the turnovers are golden brown.

***6*** While they are cooking, boil 30 g water and the remaining sugar for 5 minutes.

***7*** Remove the turnovers from the oven when they are cooked and then brush them with syrup. Leave to cool on a rack.

Serves **4** / Preparation: **25** min / Resting: **10** min / Cooking: **45** min

# UPSIDE-DOWN *apricot tart*

- 750 g/ 1lb 10 oz. firm apricots
- 50 g/¼ cup butter
- 100 g/1 cup caster sugar
- 200 g/7 oz. shortcrust pastry (see recipe p.9)

***1*** Preheat the oven to 410°F.

***2*** Rinse, dry and then pit the apricots, cut them in half.

***3*** Melt the butter and then coat it over the bottom of a non-stick cake tin. Sprinkle the bottom of the tin with sugar, then put the apricot halves on top, with the rounded side in the sugar.

***4*** Place on a medium heat for about 15 minutes until it forms a golden caramel. Remove the tin from the heat and leave to cool. Cover with shortcrust pastry, tuck the edges of the dough around the filling using the handle of a spoon.

***5*** Make a small incision in the centre of the dough. Bake for 30 minutes. Remove the tart from the oven and leave to cool for 10 minutes.

***6*** Gently slot a knife between the dough and the edges of the tin and, while the pie is still warm, turn it out in one go onto a large plate.

***7*** Enjoy warm or cold with cream, whipped cream or a ball of vanilla ice cream.

Serves **6** / Preparation: **20** min / Resting: **3** h **15** / Cooking: **45** min

# KOUGLOF

- 1 tbsp. kirsch
- 5 cl/⅕ cup of water
- 70 g/2.5 oz. raisins
- 12 g/1 tbsp. fresh yeast
- 50 cl/2 cups warm milk
- 300 g/2 ½ cups flour
- 40 g/2 tbsp. sugar
- ½ tsp. salt
- 1 egg
- 100 g/½ cup butter at room temperature + 1 knob for the pan
- 12 whole almonds
- 1 tbsp. icing sugar

***1*** Pour the kirsch into a bowl, add the raisins and the water. Cover the bowl and let the raisins rehydrate for 30 minutes.

***2*** Prepare a leaven by crumbling the yeast into the milk, add one third of the flour, stir, cover the bowl and leave to rise for 45 minutes in a warm place.

***3*** Mix the remaining flour with the sugar, salt and egg (beaten). Add the yeast. Knead for 10 minutes then add the butter cut into pieces. Knead again until the dough is nice and smooth.

***4*** Drain the raisins well and add them to the dough. Place in a bowl, cover with cling film. Leave the dough to rise for at least 1 hour in a warm place.

***5*** Grease and flour a kouglof or brioche tin. Place one almond in the bottom of each groove. Roll the dough into a ball and place it in the tin. Leave to rise for 1 hour until doubled in volume. Preheat the oven to around 320°F, then cook the mixture for 40 to 45 minutes.

***6*** Leave to cool for around ten minutes before placing a plate over the kouglof to turn it out of the tin. Sprinkle with icing sugar.

Served with a glass of wine from its native Alsace region, this raisin brioche is sure to impress. At its best on the second day, when it is a little stale.

Serves **6** / Preparation: **30** min / Resting: **14** h / Cooking: **45** min

# EGG
# *custard tart*

- 80 cl/3⅓ cups milk
- 20 cl/⅞ cup single cream
- 5 eggs
- 90 g/½ cup caster sugar
- 1 tbsp. vanilla extract
- 60 g/½ cup cornflour

For the shortcrust pastry
- 250 g/2 cups flour
- 125 g/½ cup softened butter +1 knob for the pan
- 5 g/1 tsp. salt
- 5 cl/⅕ cup water

***1*** Prepare the pastry: pour the flour into a deep bowl and make a well. In the centre, add the softened butter cut into pieces and the salt. Rub the mixture using your fingertips and then add water. Knead quickly until the dough is soft and smooth. Make the dough into a ball, wrap in cling film and leave in the refrigerator for 2 hours.

***2*** Remove the pastry from the fridge and leave to soften for 15 minutes. Preheat the oven to 350°F.

***3*** Roll out the pastry until 0.5 cm thick. Grease a tin with butter and lay out the pastry. Prick the bottom with a fork a few times, cover with a sheet of baking paper and hold in place with dried pulses or baking beads. Bake for 10 minutes then remove the weights and continue cooking for 5 minutes.

***4*** Heat the milk and cream until the mixture just begins to simmer. Beat the eggs with the sugar and vanilla extract until the mixture turns white. Stir in the cornflour and add the boiling milk and cream while whisking. Pour the mixture into a saucepan and gently bring to the boil while still whisking. When the mixture begins to simmer, remove from the heat and pour into the pastry case. Bake for 30 minutes, the flan is cooked when the dough is brown and the cream is set. Leave to cool before refrigerating overnight.

Serves **6** / Preparation: **25** min / Resting: **12** h / Cooking: **5** min

# CHOCOLATE *charlotte*

- 4 eggs
- 50 g/½ cup icing sugar
- 50 g/¼ cup lightly salted butter+1 knob for the pan
- 125 g/4 oz. dark chocolate (70% cocoa)
- 15 cl espresso
- 3 tbsp. Grand Marnier® or cognac
- 24 ladyfinger biscuits
- Custard to serve

For the topping
- 15 cl whipping cream
- 150 g/5 oz. chocolate

***1*** Break the eggs, separate the white from the yolk. Beat the egg whites until stiff. When they start to firm up, gradually add the icing sugar and keep whisking. Cut the butter and chocolate into pieces. Melt together in a simmering bain marie until the mixture is smooth and creamy. Whisk the egg yolks until frothy, add them to the melted chocolate. Then add ⅓ of the beaten egg whites, stirring vigorously, and add the rest gradually, folding gently with a spatula. Mix the coffee and alcohol of your choice in a deep dish.

***2*** Dip half the ladyfinger biscuits quickly into this mixture, then place them on the edges and bottom of the tin. Spread half the chocolate mousse over the first layer of biscuits. Dip more biscuits in the coffee and use them to make another layer. Add the remaining mousse and finish with a layer of ladyfingers soaked in coffee. Tap the tin on the worktop to pack down the contents, then place a plate on top. Refrigerate for 12 hours.

***3*** Prepare the topping: heat the whipping cream, cut up the chocolate and cover with the hot cream, stirring to produce a smooth creamy mixture.

***4*** Turn out the charlotte, coat it with chocolate and serve with custard.

Serves **6** / Preparation: **15** min / Cooking: **30** min

# CHOCOLATE *cake*

- 70 g/$\frac{3}{5}$ cup flour
- 1 tsp. baking powder
- 1 pinch salt
- 250 g/9 oz. good quality dark chocolate (min. 70% cocoa)
- 150 g/$\frac{2}{3}$ cup butter + 1 knob for the tin
- 5 eggs
- 170 g/$\frac{2}{3}$ cup caster sugar
- 1 tsp. vanilla extract

***1*** Preheat the oven to 350°F.

***2*** Mix the flour, baking powder and salt.

***3*** Chop the chocolate roughly and melt in a bain marie together with the butter cut into small pieces. Smooth out the mixture evenly with a spatula. Transfer to a large bowl. Leave to cool for a few minutes then add the eggs one by one, mixing well each time. Sprinkle in the flour, stir, then add the icing sugar and vanilla extract.

***4*** Grease a cake tin with butter and distribute the mixture evenly. Bake for 20 to 25 minutes. Be careful not to overcook the cake to keep it soft: check that it's done by sliding in the blade of a knife, it should come out without any sticky traces of mixture but still slightly moist.

***5*** Once out of the oven, let the cake rest before turning it out, still warm, onto a cooling rack.

Serves **4** to **6** / Preparation: **15** min / Cooking: **45** min

# POUND CAKE MADE WITH salted butter

- 160 g/1⅓ cups flour
- 2 tsp. baking powder
- 160 g/⅔ cup softened lightly salted butter+1 knob for the pan
- 160 g/¾ cup sugar
- 3 medium eggs

***1*** Preheat the oven to 300°F.

***2*** Mix the flour and baking powder.

***3*** Grease a cake tin with butter.

***4*** Work the butter with a fork until it takes on the consistency of a cream, then add the sugar. Mix well until smooth.

***5*** Add the eggs one by one, mixing every time. Stir in the flour gradually. When the mixture is smooth, pour it into the cake tin.

***6*** Bake for 40 to 45 minutes. Check that the cake is done by inserting the blade of a knife, it should come out clean, without any traces of mixture.

Serves **4** to **6** / Preparation: **25** min / Resting: **2** h / Cooking: **35** min

# TARTE *Tatin*

- 100 g/1.2 cup butter + 1 knob for the pan
- 2 kg/4.4 lb apples
- 200 g/1 cup caster sugar
- 1 egg for egg wash

For shortcrust pastry
- 150 g/1 ¼ cups flour
- 75 g/⅓ cup butter
- 1 pinch salt
- 2.5 cl/1.5 tbsp. water

We shall always be grateful to the Tatin sisters, who one day ruined a classic apple tart by forgetting to put the pastry in the bottom of the tin! Sometimes it doesn't take much to come up with a great recipe!

***1*** Prepare the shortcrust pastry: place the flour into a large bowl, make a well for the butter (cut into pieces) and salt. Work the mixture with the fingertips then add water. Knead quickly to form a smooth dough, make a ball and wrap it in cling film. Leave to rest for 2 hours in the refrigerator. Preheat the oven to 410°F.

***2*** Melt the butter in a small saucepan.

***3*** Peel the apples and cut into thick wedges. Grease a tin (unless using a non-stick tin), sprinkle the bottom with half the sugar and arrange the apple wedges. Sprinkle evenly with the remaining sugar and baste with melted butter. Cook over a medium heat until a golden caramel appears, then turn off the heat.

***4*** Remove the dough from the refrigerator 15 minutes before rolling it out to a thickness of 5 mm, then cut a circle the size of your tin. Place the circle over the apples. Using the handle of a teaspoon, evenly press the edges of the pastry closed around the apples. Beat the egg and glaze the top of the dough.

***5*** Bake at 410°F for 25 minutes. Leave to stand for a few minutes, then turn out the tarte.

***6*** Serve with double cream, whipped cream or vanilla ice cream.

Serves **4** / Preparation: **20** min / Cooking: **8** min

# PEACH *Melba*

- 30 g/1 oz. sliced almonds
- 4 firm peaches
- 140 g/⅔ cup caster sugar
- 1 tbsp. kirsch (alternatively rum)
- 150 g/5 oz. raspberries
- Juice of ½ lemon
- 50 cl/2 cups vanilla ice cream
- Whipped cream for decoration (optional)

***1*** Brown the almonds for a few minutes in a frying pan, without fat, then set aside.

***2*** Immerse the peaches in boiling water for 30 seconds, pass them under cold water and remove the skin. Cut them in half.

***3*** Heat 20 cl/⅞ cup water with 100 g/½ cup caster sugar, bring to the boil for 2 minutes, then add the kirsch (or rum).

***4*** Poach the peaches in this syrup for 5 minutes then drain and allow to cool completely.

***5*** Mix the raspberries (reserve a few for decoration) with the remaining sugar and the lemon juice.

***6*** Divide into 4 cups, 1 quenelle of vanilla ice cream and 1 poached peach in each, top with raspberry coulis and decorate with the sliced almonds, remaining raspberries, and whipped cream if desired.

Dessert created in 1893 by Auguste Escoffier in honour of the Australian singer Nellie Melba. This dish can be made using other fruits, particularly strawberries.

Serves **6** / Preparation: **25** min / Cooking: **45** min

# NORMAN *pear tart*

- 1 shortcrust pastry (recipe p. 9)
- 100 g/4 cups double cream
- 60 g/⅓ cup sugar
- 7 cl/¼ cup kirsch (optional)
- 1 kg/2 lb 3 oz. firm, ripe pears
- Butter and flour for the tin

***1*** Preheat the oven to 350°F.

***2*** Butter and flour a tart tin and line it with pastry. Prick the pastry base a few times with a fork. Cover with a sheet of baking paper and it hold in place with pulses or baking beads.

***3*** Bake for 10 minutes then remove the baking beads or pulses and the sheet of baking paper and continue cooking for 5 minutes.

***4*** Remove the tart base from the oven and raise the oven temperature to 400°F.

***5*** Whisk the cream with the sugar and kirsch.

***6*** Peel and core the pears, cut them in 2 lengthways and arrange them in a rosette on the base of the tart. Pour the cream over the top and bake for 30 minutes, until the tart is golden brown.

To be 100% Norman, you can prepare this tart with apples and add calvados instead of kirsch.

Serves **4** to **6** / Preparation: **45** min / Cooking: **45** min

# TARTE *aux abricots*

- 1 shortcrust pastry
- 400 g/14 oz. apricots (300 g/10 ½ oz. pitted if using frozen apricots)
- 2 eggs
- 30 cl/1 ¼ cups double cream
- 100 g/½ cup caster sugar
- 4 tbsp. ground almonds
- Butter + flour for the tin

***1*** Preheat the oven to 350°F.

***2*** Butter and flour a tart tin and lay out the pastry, prick it a few times with a fork. Place a sheet of baking paper on top and cover with pulses (split peas, dried beans) or baking beads.

***3*** Bake for 10 minutes then remove the tart base from the oven, remove the pulses and baking paper and bake for another 3 minutes. The base of the tart should be lightly browned.

***4*** Increase the oven temperature to 410°F.

***5*** Wash and dry the apricots, cut into slices.

***6*** Beat the eggs with the cream and caster sugar.

***7*** Spread the ground almonds across the tart base and arrange the apricot slices in a rosette. Pour the cream mixture over the top.

***8*** Bake for 20 to 30 minutes until the cream is set and the tart is golden.

Serves **4** / Preparation: **15** min / Cooking: **30** min

# CHERRY *clafoutis*

- 40 g/2 tbsp. butter + a little for the tin
- 30 cl/1 ¼ cups whole milk
- 1 vanilla pod (or 2 tsp vanilla extract)
- 550 g/1lb 3 oz. ripe cherries
- 4 eggs
- 80 g/⅜ cup caster sugar + 1 tbsp. for the tin
- 1 pinch of salt
- 80 g/⅜ cup flour
- 2 tbsp. icing sugar (optional)

Leave the cherry stones in the clafoutis. You'll be following the traditional Limousin recipe, and your dessert will be even better because the cherries make less juice.

***1*** Preheat the oven to 410°F.

***2*** Cut the butter into small cubes.

***3*** Pour the milk into a pan, open the vanilla pod, scrape the inside into the pan using the tip of a small knife, then place the pod in the milk. Gently bring to the boil and then turn off the flame. Add the butter, mix until melted, and cover. Leave to infuse during the preparation time.

***4*** After removing their stalks, rinse and dry the cherries.

***5*** Whisk the eggs with the sugar and salt until the mixture whitens. Add the flour and then gradually pour in the warm milk, whisking gently (remove the vanilla pod beforehand).

***6*** Butter a gratin dish, sprinkle the bottom with sugar. Pour the mixture into the dish. Bake for 10 minutes at 410°F then lower the temperature to 350°F and continue cooking for 20 minutes until the surface is golden brown.

***7*** Remove the clafoutis from the oven, sprinkle with icing sugar. Enjoy warm or cold.

Serves **4** to **6** / Preparation: **25** to **35** min (depending on the version) / Cooking: **45** min

# TARTE au citron

- 1 sweet pastry
- 3 untreated lemons
- 100 g/½ cup unsalted butter, soft
- 200 g/1 cup caster sugar
- 4 eggs
- Icing sugar for decoration
- Butter + flour for the tin

For a meringue version:
- 2 egg whites
- 2 tbsp. icing sugar

The classic version can be seen in every bakery in France. You will also find it reworked in patisseries run by the great chefs and on the tables of the finest restaurants.

**1** Preheat the oven to 350°F. Butter and flour a tart tin and lay out the pastry, prick it a few times with a fork. Place a sheet of baking paper on top and cover with pulses (split peas, dried beans) or baking beads. Bake for 10 minutes until the edges start to turn golden. Remove the pulses or baking beads and baking paper and bake for another 3 minutes.

**2** Prepare the lemon cream: rinse and dry 1 lemon, then grate the zest. Squeeze all 3 lemons, you must end up with 15 cl of juice, add a little cold water if necessary.

**3** Beat the soft butter with the sugar and lemon zest until you get a cream, then add the eggs one by one. When the mixture is nice and smooth, gradually add the lemon juice – keep stirring. Pour the mixture into the tart base. Gently shake the tin to distribute the cream evenly. Bake for about 30 minutes. Let the tart cool a little, then turn it out and leave to fully cool on a rack. This tart can be served just sprinkled with a little icing sugar or in a meringue version.

**4** Meringue version: whisk the whites gently with an electric whisk until they begin to foam and then increase the speed. When the whites begin to firm, add the icing sugar and keep whisking until the whole mixture is firm enough to form peaks. Pour all the mixture into a piping bag with a nozzle (you can also distribute the whites with a spatula) and then pipe the meringue onto the tart. Place under the grill for 1 to 2 minutes until the top is golden brown.

For **4** tartlets or **8** minitartlets / Preparation: **50** min / Resting: **1** h / Cooking: **35** min

# STRAWBERRY *tartlets*

- 25 cl/1 cup milk
- ½ vanilla pod
- 2 egg yolks
- 60 g/¼ cup caster sugar
- 30 g/¼ cup flour + a little for the tin
- 80 g/⅜ cup redcurrant jelly
- 1 sweet pastry (see recipe p. 9)
- 400 g/14 oz. strawberries
- Butter for the tin

***1*** For the crème pâtissière: Pour the milk into a saucepan. Split the vanilla pod and scrape the insides into the pan, also add the pod to the milk. Bring to the boil.
***2*** Whisk the egg yolks with the sugar until they turn white, then add the flour. Pour in the hot vanilla milk while whisking (remove the pod beforehand). Transfer the mixture to a saucepan and thicken over a low heat, stirring constantly for about 8 to 10 minutes.
***3*** Pour the cream into another container and let it cool completely, stirring often.
***4*** For the topping: Melt the redcurrant jelly over a low heat, adding 1 tablespoon of water. Pour the mixture into a container and allow to cool completely. Butter and flour 4 tartlet tins 10 cm in diameter.
***5*** Preheat the oven to 410°F. Lightly flour the work surface and a rolling pin and roll the pastry to a thickness of about 4 to 5 mm. Line the tins with pastry, pierce the bottom a few times with a fork. Cover the tart bases with a piece of baking paper, fill with pulses (or baking beads). Bake for 10 minutes, remove the paper and pulses, bake for 20 minutes. The tartlets must be cooked and golden.
***6*** Turn them out gently and leave to cool on a rack.
***7*** Remove their stalks, then rinse and dry the strawberries. Divide the crème pâtissière into the tartlet cases and add the strawberries. Glaze the strawberries with the syrup using a pastry brush.

Serves **4** / Preparation: **30** min / Resting: **12** h **15** / Cooking: **2** h

# VACHERIN
## with red berries

- 3 egg whites
- 180 g/⅞ cup caster sugar
- 12 cl/½ cup cream (preferably whipping cream)
- 350 g/12 oz. mixed red berries (redcurrants, raspberries, strawberries)
- 30 cl/1¼ cup vanilla ice cream

***1*** Prepare the meringues the day before: preheat the oven to 410°F.
***2*** Whisk the egg whites gently with an electric mixer. When they begin to foam, increase the speed. Once they become firm, gradually add 150 g caster sugar and whisk for 1 more minute.
***3*** Line 2 baking sheets with baking paper. Using a spoon or a piping bag, make 8 meringue circles about 10 cm in diameter.
***4*** Bake for 2 hours. During the first hour of cooking, open the oven door 3 or 4 times for a few seconds to let out the moisture. Turn off the oven and leave the meringues to cool inside.
***5*** The next day: pour the cream into a bowl (preferably metal). Place the bowl and the blades of the whisk in the freezer for 15 minutes.
***6*** Remove their stalks, then wash and dry the red berries, cut the strawberries into pieces.
***7*** Mix 100 g red berries with 15 g caster sugar and 5 cl water.
***8*** Whip the cream, starting on slow speed and then accelerating. When the cream is stiff, keep whipping and add the remaining sugar little by little. Pour it into a piping bag with a nozzle.
***9*** Arrange the layers: scoop out 4 balls of ice cream with an ice cream scoop, place them in the centre of 4 disks of meringues. Distribute the fruit around and on top of the ice cream (reserve a little for decoration). Place a second meringue disk on top, press lightly to make it stick. Place the cream on top, drizzle with coulis and decorate with the remaining red berries. Serve immediately.

Serves **6** / Preparation: **30** min / Resting: **1** h **15** / Cooking: **30** min

# RUM *baba*

- 10 g/1 level tbsp. baker's yeast or brewer's yeast
- 75 cl/3 cups milk
- 4 eggs
- 90 g/½ cup butter + a little for the tin
- 250 g/2 cups flour
- . tsp. fine salt
- 25 g/2 tbsp. caster sugar

For chantilly cream:
- 25 cl/1 cup whipping cream
- 1 vanilla pod
- 25 g/¼ cup icing sugar

For the syrup:
- 325 g/1½ cups caster sugar
- 30 cl/1¼ cup water
- 1 untreated lemon zest
- 8 cl/⅓ cup amber rum

Nicolas Stohrer invented the rum baba in 1835. Today, in the pastry shop that bears his name, at 51 rue Montorgueuil (75002 Paris), you can sample a rum baba prepared according to the original recipe.

***1*** Dissolve the yeast in 10 cl warm milk. Whisk the whole eggs. Melt the butter.
***2*** Sift the flour into a bowl, make a well in the centre and pour in the yeast mixture. Add the salt and sugar. Knead the mixture by hand or using a mixer, gradually incorporating the beaten eggs and then the remaining milk. Add the warm melted butter. Work the dough well until it detaches from the edges of the bowl. Cover the dough with cling film and leave to stand at room temperature for 30 minutes.
***3*** Butter a savarin mould.
***4*** Mix the dough with a wooden spoon and transfer to the mould. The mixture should half fill the tin. Leave to stand again for about 30 minutes until the dough doubles in volume.
***5*** Preheat the oven to 350°F. Bake for 25 to 30 minutes until the surface is golden brown.
***6*** Turn out the baba and leave to cool on a rack.
***7*** Prepare the chantilly cream: pour the cream into a bowl (preferably metal), split the vanilla pod and scrape the insides into the cream. Stir, then place the bowl and the blades of the whisk in the freezer for 15 minutes.
***8*** Meanwhile, prepare the syrup: pour the sugar, water and lemon zest into a saucepan. Bring to the boil, simmer for 5 minutes then add the rum.
***9*** Pour the syrup onto the baba so that it absorbs well.
***10*** Whip the cream, adding the icing sugar gradually. Apply the chantilly to the centre of the baba using a piping bag with a nozzle, or a spoon.
***11*** Serve plain or decorated with fresh or candied fruit.

Serves **6** / Preparation: **30** min / Resting: **30** min / Cooking: **30** min

# FRANGIPANE
## *king cake*

- 600 g/21 oz. puff pastry (puff pastry recipe p. 12)
- 100 g/½ cup butter at room temperature
- 125 g/⅔ cup caster sugar
- 3 whole eggs + 1 yolk
- 5 g/¼ cup rum
- 60 g/½ cup flour
- 125 g/⅔ cup ground almonds
- 1 broad bean

***1*** Roll out the puff pastry 3 to 4 mm thick so that you can cut 2 circles 24 cm in diameter. Keep the pastry circles cool during preparation time.

***2*** Work the soft butter with the sugar to get a smooth cream. Add the whole eggs one by one, mixing well each time, then add the rum. Stir in the flour and then the ground almonds.

***3*** Beat the egg yolk.

***4*** Spread the cream mixture on to one of the circles of dough, leaving a border of 2.5 cm, then place the bean on top. Brush a little egg yolk on the side of the dough and place the second circle of dough on top of the filling. Press the edges to seal the cake together.

***5*** Brush the top and sides of the cake with the egg yolk. Score crosses on the surface using the tip of a knife, without cutting into the dough.

***6*** Chill for 30 minutes then brush the surface with the remaining egg yolk.

***7*** Preheat the oven to 410°F. Bake for 25 to 30 minutes until the pastry is golden brown. Enjoy warm or cold.

King cakes are eaten on January 6th for Epiphany, a Christian feast celebrating the visit of the Magi to Jesus. You can give this traditional cake a modern touch by preparing it with apples, pistachio, chocolate, etc.

Serves **6** / Preparation: **45** min / Cooking: **30** min

# PROFITEROLES

- 1 choux pastry (see recipe p. 10)
- 200 g/7 oz. dark chocolate
- 10 cl/2/5 cup single cream
- 10 cl/2/5 cup milk
- 50 cl/2 cups vanilla ice cream

***1*** Prepare the dough by following the recipe on p. 10 but stop before baking.

***2*** Preheat the oven to 410°F. Line a baking sheet with baking paper.

***3*** Make the dough into circles about 3 cm wide and 2 cm high, spacing them 3 cm apart. Use a piping bag with a nozzle to make the choux.

***4*** Lightly press the top of the choux with a fork soaked in water.

***5*** Slip a small bowl of water in the bottom of the oven and bake the choux for about 20 minutes until they are puffy and golden (do not open the oven door during cooking).

***6*** Remove the choux gently and let them cool completely on a rack.

***7*** Prepare the chocolate sauce: roughly chop the chocolate. Heat the cream and milk until it boils, then pour it over the chocolate. Stir gently until the sauce is smooth. Keep this sauce warm in a bain-marie.

***8*** When the choux are cold, cut them in half and fill with vanilla ice cream. Portion on plates and drizzle with chocolate sauce.

***9*** Serve immediately while the ice cream is cold and the sauce is hot.

It was Antonin Carême, the nineteenth century "cook of kings and king of cooks", who glorified choux pastry with the idea of filling it with crème pâtissière or whipped cream. And so the profiterole was born...

Serves **4** to **6** / Preparation: **35** min / Resting: **2** h **30** / Cooking: **35** min

# TARTE au chocolat

- Flour
- Butter
- 1 heaped tbsp. cocoa powder

For sweet pastry:
- 180 g/1 ½ cups flour
- 85 g/²⁄₅ cup butter
- 90 g/⅔ cup icing sugar
- 2 egg yolks

For the ganache:
- 200 g/7 oz. dark chocolate, minimum 70% cocoa
- 8 cl/⅓ cup milk
- 20 cl/⅞ cup single cream
- 1 large egg

***1*** Prepare the dough: sift the flour into a bowl, make a well.
***2*** Cut the butter into small pieces, place them in the well.
***3*** First mix by hand to coat the pieces of butter in flour, then rub the dough with your fingertips. Add the other ingredients and rub together quickly to form a smooth ball.
***4*** Flatten this ball into a thick patty, wrap it in cling film, store in a cool place for 2 hours.
***5*** Remove the dough from the refrigerator 15 minutes before rolling out. Preheat the oven to 350°F. Butter and flour a tart tin.
***6*** Flour a rolling pin and the work surface and roll out the dough carefully.
***7*** Line the tin with pastry. Run the rolling pin around the edges of the tin to remove excess pastry. Prick the tart base a few times. Place a sheet of baking paper on top, hold in place with baking beads. Bake for 10 minutes, then remove the weights and baking paper and bake for another 5 minutes. Increase the oven temperature to 370°F.
***8*** Prepare the ganache: roughly chop the chocolate with a knife, place it in a heat-resistant container.
***9*** Gently beat the egg. Pour the milk and cream into a saucepan, stir, then bring to the boil. Pour over the chocolate. Leave to cool for a few minutes and then add the egg.
***10*** Pour the mixture into the tart base, smooth the surface with a spatula.
***11*** Bake the tart in the middle of the oven for 12 to 15 minutes, the cream must be firm but still a little wobbly in the centre. Remove the tart from the oven and leave to cool on a rack.
***12*** Sprinkle with cocoa powder. Serve at room temperature.

Serves **4** / Preparation: **40** min / Resting: **15** min / Cooking: **15** min

# FRAISIER *cake*

- 15 g/1 tbsp. melted butter
- 100 g/¾ cup flour
- 3 eggs
- 110 g/½ cup caster sugar
- 1 pinch of salt
- 20 cl/⅞ cup whipping cream
- 40 g/1½ oz. mascarpone
- 450 g/1 lb strawberries
- 180 g/6 oz. strawberry jam

This dessert will delight you with its soft, velvety sponge and crisp strawberries. Only fresh fruit gives this cake the delicate taste of summer.

***1*** Preheat the oven to 410°F. Line a baking sheet with baking paper and butter it with a pastry brush.
***2*** Sieve the flour. Break the eggs, separating the whites from the yolks.
***3*** Whisk the yolks with 100 g sugar and the salt until the mixture whitens. Gradually add the sifted flour while whisking.
***4*** Whisk the whites into firm peaks and then fold them quickly into the previous preparation, delicately lifting the mixture with a spatula.
***5*** Pour the mixture onto the baking sheet, shake slightly to distribute it evenly, and then smooth the surface with a spatula.
***6*** Bake for 12 to 15 minutes until the sponge is golden brown. Let it cool and then cut into 8 equal rectangles.
***7*** Pour the cream into a bowl (preferably metal). Place the bowl and the blades of the whisk in the freezer.
***8*** Whip the mascarpone to soften it.
***9*** Whip the cream, when it becomes firm, add the remaining sugar.
***10*** Gently fold the mascarpone into the whipped cream, lifting with a spatula.
***11*** Remove their stalks and wash the strawberries. Cut into 2, or 4 if they are very large.
***12*** Spread the strawberry jam on the rectangles of sponge cake.
***13*** Top half of the rectangles with half of the cream, then add half of the strawberries.
***14*** Place the rest of the sponge on top, cover with cream and strawberries.

For **10** to **12** eclairs / Preparation: **1** h **30** / Cooking: **1** h

# CHOCOLATE eclairs

- 1 choux pastry (recipe p. 10)

For the icing:
- 1 sheet of gelatine
- 55 g/¼ cup caster sugar
- 45 cl/2 cups water
- 20 g/⅛ cup cocoa powder
- 35 cl/1 ½ cup whipping cream

For chocolate creme patissiere:

- 100 g/3 ½ oz. dark chocolate, 70% cocoa, chopped
- 75 cl/3 cups milk
- 5 egg yolks
- 170 g/¾ cup caster sugar
- 60 g/½ cup corn starch
- 70 g/⅓ cup butter at room temperature, cut into pieces

***1*** Prepare the icing: soak the gelatine in cold water. Pour the sugar, water, cocoa and cream into a saucepan and bring to a boil, whisking gently. Drain the gelatine. Remove the saucepan from the heat and add the gelatine. Pour the mixture into a bowl, allow to cool, then cover with cling film and refrigerate until completely cold.
***2*** Prepare the crème pâtissière: place the chocolate in a bowl. Heat the milk until it boils. Whisk the eggs with sugar and corn starch for 3 minutes. Add the milk, while whisking. Pour the mixture into the saucepan and thicken the cream over a low heat, stirring constantly. Pour the hot cream over the chocolate, stir until the mixture is smooth. Leave to cool. Add the butter at room temperature then cover with cling film and refrigerate.
***3*** Prepare choux pastry (recipe p. 10). Preheat the oven to 410°F. Line a baking sheet with baking paper.
***4*** Pour the choux pastry into a piping bag with a nozzle (diameter 15 to 18 cm). Make the eclairs 10 to 12 cm long. Score the surface with a fork soaked in cold water.
***5*** Bake in the middle of the oven for 20 to 25 minutes, without opening the oven door until the eclairs are evenly browned (even in the grooves). Remove the eclairs from the oven and leave to cool on a rack. Prepare the next batch.
***6*** Cut the eclairs in half, lengthways. Remove the icing from the refrigerator, heat in a bain marie to 95°F. Transfer to a dish. Dip the top of the eclairs into the icing and smooth.
***7*** Remove the crème pâtissière from the refrigerator, whisk until soft, then apply to the bottom half of the eclairs.
***8*** Close the eclairs, let the icing harden, then enjoy.

For **4** tartlets / Preparation: **15** min / Cooking: **40** min

# WALNUT *tartlets*

- 1 sweet pastry (see recipe p. 9)
- 10 cl/$\frac{2}{5}$ cup whipping cream
- 50 g/¼ cup salted butter (or 50 g/¼ cup unsalted butter + 2 g/⅓ tsp. salt)
- 140 g/⅔ cup caster sugar
- 220 g/7 ½ oz. walnut kernels
- Butter and flour for tins.

***1*** Preheat the oven to 350°F.

***2*** Butter 4 tartlet tins. Roll out the pastry and cut 4 circles to the dimensions of your tins. Line the tins with pastry, pierce the bottom a few times with a fork. Cover the tart bases with a piece of baking paper, fill with pulses (or baking beads). Bake for 10 minutes, remove the pulses or baking beads and baking paper. Bake for another 20 minutes. Turn out the tart bases gently and leave to cool on a rack.

***3*** Heat the cream in a small saucepan. Cut the butter into small pieces. Pour the caster sugar into a saucepan. Soak it in a little water over a medium heat, stirring gently from time to time. When the mixture has a beautiful amber colour, stop cooking. Pour in a small amount of cream and dilute. Add the cream gradually. Add the butter and stir, transfer to a heat resistant bowl.

***4*** Set aside 3 tablespoons of caramel. Pour the walnut kernels into the caramel and stir well to coat all the nuts.

***5*** Divide the mixture between the tart bases and sprinkle with the remaining caramel. Allow to cool before eating.

Makes a **dozen** fritters / Preparation: **35** min / Resting: **1** h **45** / Cooking: **20** min

# SWEET *fritters*

- 8 g/1 heaped tsp. yeast
- 2 tbsp. milk at room temperature
- 250 g/2 cups flour+1 tbsp.
- 40 g/2 level tbsp. caster sugar
- 1 pinch salt
- 2 eggs
- 1 tbsp. orange blossom
- 1 tsp. lemon zest
- 60 g/¼ cup softened butter
- Frying oil
- 3 tbsp. icing sugar

**1** Crumble the yeast into the milk and leave to stand for 10 minutes.

**2** Mix the flour, sugar, and salt in a large bowl, add the beaten eggs, yeast, orange blossom and lemon zest. Knead, then add the butter cut into pieces. Knead again for 15 minutes, until the dough is nice and soft. Make the dough into a ball and place it into a deep bowl. Cover the bowl with cling film and leave to stand for 30 minutes at room temperature.

**3** Flour the work surface and rolling pin. Roll out the pastry to a thickness of 2 cm. Using a serrated pastry wheel, cut rectangles of 7x4 cm, make an indentation in the middle. Place the rectangles on a sheet of baking paper and leave to rise for another 30 minutes, again covered with cling film.

**4** To ensure the fritters hold their shape, place them in the refrigerator for 15 minutes to firm the dough before frying.

**5** Prepare a pan of hot oil and fry the fritters until golden, turning once halfway through cooking.

**6** Drain on paper towels. Serve the fritters sprinkled with icing sugar.

These fritters, originally from Lyon, were traditionally made and eaten on feast days, especially for Mardi Gras.

Makes **20** macarons / Preparation: **45** min / Cooking: **20** min / Resting: around **20** min

# MACARONS

For coffee buttercream
- 150 g/⅔ cup butter at room temperature
- 4 egg yolks
- 6 cl/⅕ cup of water
- 150 g/⅔ cup caster sugar
- A few drops of coffee extract

For chocolate buttercream
- 150 g/⅔ cup butter at room temperature
- 4 egg yolks
- 150 g/⅔ cup caster sugar
- 75 g/2.5 oz. dark chocolate (70% cocoa)

For the shells
- 75 g/⅔ cup icing sugar
- 75 g/2.5 oz. powdered almonds
- 2 medium egg whites
- Powdered food colouring, coffee and chocolate (optional)
- 75 g/⅓ cup caster sugar

***1*** Prepare the coffee buttercream: work the butter with a fork until it has a creamy consistency. Beat the egg yolks in a bowl. Pour the sugar and water into a pan, heat to 233°F to produce a syrup.

***2*** Drizzle the hot syrup over the egg yolks while whisking. Keep whisking until the mixture has completely cooled and tripled in size. Add the creamed butter and the coffee extract. Mix well until smooth. Leave the mixture to cool and refrigerate. Repeat the process for the chocolate buttercream, substituting the coffee extract with chocolate, simply melted in a bain marie without overheating.

***3*** Prepare the macaron shells: mix together the icing sugar and almond powder. Add an egg white, and a drop of food colouring if desired, and leave to rest. Beat the second egg white until stiff. Pour the caster sugar into a saucepan, add a few drops of water. Heat to 240°F. Then drizzle the syrup over the egg white, beating until the mixture forms peaks. Gently fold the egg white into the icing sugar/almond powder mixture.

***4*** Pour the mixture into a pastry bag. Line 2 baking trays with baking paper and pipe out the macarons in small circles 4 cm in diameter, spacing well. Preheat the oven to 300°F. Let your macarons dry for 20 minutes, then bake for 12 minutes. Open the oven door twice during cooking to let the moisture escape. Remove the macarons from the baking tray and assemble with either coffee or chocolate buttercream.

Makes **24** madeleines // Preparation: **20** min // Resting: **12** h // Cooking: **15** min

# MADELEINES

- 150 g/⅔ cup lightly salted butter+15 g/1 tbsp. for the tins
- 5 eggs
- 150 g/⅔ cup caster sugar
- 150 g/1¼ cups flour
- 1 tbsp. orange blossom water

***1*** Preheat the oven to 460°F.

***2*** Gently melt the butter over a low heat.

3 Break the eggs and separate the whites from the yolks. Beat the egg whites until stiff.

***4*** Beat the yolks with sugar until pale, add the melted butter, sprinkle in the flour and add the orange blossom water. Whisk well to give a light mixture and gently fold in the egg whites, lifting with a spatula. Let the dough rest for at least 12 hours (preferably 24 hours).

***5*** Grease 2 twelve-cup madeleine tins and fill with the mixture. Bake at 460°F for 5 minutes then turn down the oven to 410°F and cook for another 10 minutes.

***6*** Turn out the madeleines while hot and leave to cool on a rack.

A sweet treat originally from Commercy in Lorraine, the madeleine owes its popularity to Marcel Proust.

Serves **1** / Preparation: **5** min / Resting: **1** h **30** / Cooking: **2** h **10**

# FRENCH TOAST WITH HOMEMADE caramel spread

- 1 tin condensed milk
- 1 egg
- 15 cl/$\frac{5}{8}$ cup milk
- 1 tsp. sugar
- 15 g/1 tbsp. butter
- 1 dash of oil
- 2 thick slices stale bread
- 1 sachet vanilla sugar

***1*** Prepare the caramel spread: place the tin of condensed milk in a saucepan and cover well with water. Bring to the boil and cook for 2 hours, making sure that the tin is always submerged. After cooking, remove the tin from the pan and leave to cool completely before opening (danger of burns). Then open the tin, pour the contents into a large bowl and work with a fork to make a smooth cream. Put the cream in a glass jar.

***2*** Whisk the egg with the milk and sugar.

***3*** Heat the butter and oil in a frying pan. Dip the bread in milk on both sides until just moistened. Brown the slices of bread in the butter, turning halfway through cooking.

***4*** Sprinkle with vanilla sugar and eat hot or warm with your homemade caramel spread.

***5*** Keep the caramel spread refrigerated in a sealed jar and consume within 5 days.

This dessert, once seen as food for the poor, since it used up stale bread that would otherwise be thrown away, has been rediscovered and is now served at top restaurants.

For around **20** small meringues / Preparation: **20** min / Resting: **24** h / Cooking: **50** min

# MERINGUE

- 2 eggs
- 50 g/¼ cup caster sugar

**1** Preheat the oven to 210°F.

**2** Line the baking sheet with baking paper.

**3** Break the eggs separating the whites from the yolks (save the yolks for another use). Whisk the whites gently until they begin to foam, then whisk vigorously (preferably with an electric whisk). When the whites start to firm up, add the caster sugar little by little, and keep whipping for about 2 minutes. (To avoid sticky meringues, whites should not be beaten too long and should not be too firm.)

**4** Pour the mixture into a piping bag with a large nozzle, or use a spoon.

**5** Make small swirls on the baking sheet, spacing them slightly.

**6** Bake for 10 minutes. During the first hour of cooking, open the oven door for a few seconds every 20 minutes to remove moisture, as the meringues must "dry".

**7** Turn off the oven and allow the meringues to cool for several hours (ideally overnight) in the oven.

The short list of ingredients (just two) is no guarantee of success - so follow the recipe carefully.

For **15** financiers / Preparation: **15** min / Cooking: **20** min

# FINANCIERS

- 150 g/⅔ cup butter + a little for the tin
- 50 g/⅓ cup flour + a little for the tin
- 80 g/⅜ cup ground almonds
- 3 egg whites
- 150 g/1 ½ cups icing sugar

***1*** Preheat the oven to 350°F.

***2*** Butter and flour a tin for 15 financiers.

***3*** Cut the butter into equal cubes, place the cubes in a saucepan and melt over a medium heat. When the butter begins to melt, whisk until it starts to turn golden and has a nutty fragrance.

***4*** Filter the butter through a fine sieve and leave to cool.

***5*** Mix the flour and ground almonds. Whisk the egg whites until they begin to foam. Add the icing sugar, then the flour and almond mixture, and finally the butter.

***6*** Divide the mixture between the moulds. Bake for 15 minutes. Turn out the financiers and leave to cool on a rack.

This cake owes its shape (an ingot) and its name (the financier) to the pastry chef Lasne. In 1890 he brought the cakes then known as visitandines back into fashion. His shop was located in Paris, near the Stock Exchange, and his clients were… financiers.

For **15** macaroons / Preparation: **45** min / Cooking: **45** min

# COCONUT *macaroons*

- 30 g/2 tbsp. butter
- 150 g/¾ cup caster sugar
- 200 g/3⅓ cups grated coconut
- 3 egg whites

***1*** Preheat the oven to 350°F.

***2*** Melt the butter.

***3*** Mix the sugar and grated coconut.

***4*** Whisk the egg whites gently until they foam, then add the sugar / coconut mix, followed by the melted butter. Work the mixture until it is compact enough to be shaped.

***5*** Line a baking sheet with baking paper.

***6*** Form the mixture into 15 balls, arrange them on the baking sheet. Bake for 15 to 20 minutes until the macaroons are golden brown.

***7*** Remove them from the oven and leave to cool on the baking sheet.

For **12** cannelés / Preparation: **20** min / Resting: **12** to **24** h / Cooking: **50** min

# CANNELÉS

- 50 cl/2 cups whole milk
- 1 vanilla pod
- 50 g/¼ cup unsalted butter
- 1 tbsp. vanilla extract (optional)
- 125 g/1 cup flour
- 225 g/1⅛ cup caster sugar
- 1 pinch of salt
- 2 eggs + 2 yolks
- 7 cl/¼ cup rum

For the moulds:
- 30 g/2 tbsp. soft butter
- 50 g/⅓ cup brown or demerara sugar

The cannelé is a specialty of Bordeaux, but its origins are controversial. It dates from the fourteenth or sixteenth century, and perhaps originated in Limoges.

***1*** Pour the milk into a saucepan. Split the vanilla pod in two, scrape the inside into the pan using the tip of a small knife.

***2*** Add the pod as well as the butter and vanilla extract.

***3*** Heat gently. When the mixture begins to simmer, turn off the heat. Remove the vanilla pod and set it aside.

***4*** Mix the flour, sugar and salt. Add the whole eggs and yolks one by one, diluting with a little hot milk. Stir until the mixture is smooth and gradually add the remaining warm milk while whisking gently. Allow to cool, then add the rum and vanilla pod. Cover with cling film and chill for 12 to 24 hours.

***5*** Carefully coat each mould with soft butter. Sprinkle with brown sugar, turning the moulds several times so that their entire surface is covered. Place the moulds in the freezer for 10 to 15 minutes.

***6*** Preheat the oven to 400°F.

***7*** Remove the vanilla pod from the mixture. Whisk gently to smooth the mixture and then pour it into the moulds. Each mould should be 2/3 full. Bake the cannelés at the bottom of the oven and cook for 45 to 50 minutes. Remove the cannelés from the oven and immediately turn them out on a rack. Allow to cool completely before eating.

Tip: You can keep the mixture in the refrigerator for up to 3 days and cook your cannelés when you want them.

For about **25** truffles / Preparation: **30** min / Resting: **6** h / Cooking: **5** min

# CHOCOLATE *truffles*

- 350 g/12 oz. dark chocolate, minimum 70% cocoa
- 15 cl/⅝ cup single cream
- 15 g/⅝ cup liquid honey
- 35 g/2 ½ tbsp. butter, diced
- 4 cl/2 ½ tbsp. rum or cognac (optional)
- 60 g/½ cup cocoa powder

**1** Roughly chop the chocolate, arrange it in a heat resistant container.

**2** Pour the cream into a saucepan, add the honey. Bring to the boil while mixing. Pour the hot cream over the chocolate, gently whisk the mixture until the chocolate is melted and the ganache is smooth. Add the butter, and the rum or cognac if desired.

**3** Cover with cling film and refrigerate for 6 hours.

**4** Remove the ganache from the refrigerator. Pour the cocoa powder into a bowl.

**5** Take a walnut-sized piece of ganache on a teaspoon. Using your hands, roll it quickly into a ball and then through the cocoa powder. Arrange the truffles on a plate or in paper cases.

**6** Serve straight from the fridge.

Originally, the chocolate truffle consisted only of cream, vanilla and chocolate. Today, it is a French classic that can be reworked in many ways.

For about **35** biscuits / Preparation: **20** min / Cooking: **15** min

# ALMOND *biscuits*

- 2 egg whites
- 100 g/½ cup caster sugar
- 1 pinch of salt
- 50 g/⅓ cup flour
- 80 g/3 oz. sliced almonds
- 50 g/¼ cup melted butter

***1*** Preheat the oven to 300°F.

***2*** Whip the egg whites with the sugar and salt until the mixture begins to foam. Gradually add the sifted flour then the melted butter.

***3*** Line a baking sheet with baking paper. Using a small spoon, make small rounds of dough, spacing them well. Flatten the biscuits as thin as possible with the back of a tablespoon soaked in cold water, giving them a rounded shape. Top with almonds.

***4*** Bake in the middle of the oven for about 15 minutes until golden brown.

***5*** Turn off the oven. Remove the biscuits from the tray one by one while still hot and place on a rolling pin to give them a curved shape. Leave to cool on a rack.

***6*** Store the biscuits in a cool, dry place in an airtight, metal box.

***7*** Serve with tea, coffee or a dessert like sabayon or chocolate mousse.

For around **20** biscuits / Preparation: **20** min / Cooking: **12** min

# LANGUES de chat

- 50 g/¼ cup butter, diced, at room temperature
- 50 g/½ cup icing sugar
- 50 g/⅓ cup flour
- 1 egg white

***1*** Preheat the oven to 350°F.

***2*** Whisk the butter and icing sugar until the mixture is even and creamy. Add the vanilla extract. Gradually sift the flour into the mixture while stirring.

***3*** Vigorously whisk in half the beaten egg whites until the cream is smooth, then gently fold in the remaining half using a spatula.

***4*** Line a baking sheet with baking paper.

***5*** Put the mixture in a piping bag with a smooth nozzle (6 mm), and pipe 6 cm long sticks with 5 cm spacing.

***6*** Bake for 10 to 12 minutes until the edges are golden brown.

***7*** Remove the biscuits with a spatula, leave to cool on a rack.

***8*** These biscuits can be stored in a sealed, preferably metallic, container for several days.

For about **20** beignets / Preparation: **15** min / Resting: **1** h / Cooking: **10** min

# APPLE *beignets*

- 200 g/1⅔ cups flour
- 4 g/½ level tbsp. fresh baker's yeast
- 1 tbsp. sunflower oil
- 1 tbsp. orange flower water
- 1 egg white
- Oil for frying
- 4 apples
- Juice of 1 lemon
- 2 tbsp. caster sugar

***1*** Pour the flour into a bowl, make a well in the centre, crumble in the yeast and add the oil. Pour in about 15 cl warm water, gradually stirring until the mixture has the consistency of a pancake batter. Flavour with orange blossom water. Gently beat the egg white and fold it into the mixture with a spatula. Cover the container and leave to stand for 1 hour at room temperature.

***2*** Heat the oil in a fryer or a high-sided frying pan.

***3*** Peel the apples and drizzle with lemon juice. Core the apples with an apple corer. Cut into slices ½ cm thick. When the oil is hot, dip each slice of apple into the beignet dough, using two forks. Shake slightly, and then plunge the apples into the oil. Remove the beignets from the frying pan when golden, drain on absorbent paper and sprinkle with sugar.

For about **35** chouquettes / Preparation: **40** min / Cooking: **50** min

# CHOUQUETTE

- 1 choux pastry (see recipe p. 10)
- 4 tbsp. nib sugar

***1*** Prepare the choux pastry (see recipe p. 10).

***2*** Preheat the oven to 410°F.

***3*** Line a baking sheet, place small spoonfuls of dough 3 cm apart (or use a piping bag with a 10 mm nozzle for more regular chouquettes), sprinkle with nib sugar.

***4*** Bake for 10 minutes without opening the oven door. Lower the temperature to 350°C and continue cooking for another 15 minutes, without opening the oven door, until the choux are evenly browned.

***5*** Remove the chouquettes from the oven and leave to cool on a rack.

Light, airy and sweet… chouquettes are perfect for breakfast!

For **12** shortbread / Preparation: **35** min / Resting: **1** h **15** / Cooking: **15** min

# CHOCOLATE shortbread

For the shortbread:
- 250 g/2 cups flour
- 1 pinch of salt
- 125 g/½ cup butter at room temperature
- 100 g/½ cup sugar
- 1 egg

For the ganache:
- 100 g/3 ½ oz. dark chocolate, 70% cocoa
- 100 g/4 cups single cream
- 40 g/¼ cup caster sugar

***1*** Prepare the dough: place the flour and salt in a bowl, add the butter by rubbing the dough with your fingertips. Add the sugar, the whole egg and 6cl of water. First mix with a spatula then with your fingertips, quickly until the dough is smooth. Form a ball of dough and leave to rest for 1 hour in the fridge.

***2*** Preheat the oven to 350°F.

***3*** Remove the dough from the refrigerator 10 to 15 minutes before rolling out.

***4*** Roll the dough thinly and cut 24 shortbread slices with a cookie cutter. Bake for 12 to 15 minutes until the biscuits are golden, then let them cool on a rack.

***5*** Chop the chocolate.

***6*** Heat the cream with the sugar until it dissolves.

***7*** Pour the hot cream over the chocolate and stir until melted. Spread the chocolate mixture onto the biscuits and assemble them.

# ACKNOWLEDGEMENTS

**Julie Soucail** would like to thank the following brands for their loans of equipment, crockery and linen:

Kenwood for its superb Kmix and robot multipro compact FPM 250: www.kenwoodworld.com
Merci: www.merci-merci.com
Seletti: www.seletti.it
Variopinte: www.variopinte.com
Otsuki sama: www.otsuki-sama.com
Serax: www.serax.com
My little day: www.mylittleday.fr
Angèle des montagnes: www.angeldesmontagnes.com
Caravane: www.caravane.fr
Maisons du Monde: www.maisonsdumonde.com
Habitat: www.habitat.fr
Le Creuset: www.lecreuset.fr
Bloomingville: www.bloomingville.com
Debuyer for the loan and the quality of its products. You will find all the utensils and equipment you need for these recipes at www.debuyer.com/en

**Laurent Valentinuz** would like to thank Bruno Leprieur; Julie Soucail, the author of the recipes; the team at the librairie des Abbesses in Paris, and of course the publisher, Marie Baumann, without whom these books would never have existed.

Graphic design: Stéphanie Boulay
Translation: Ruth Clarke
Layout and editorial assistance: Sophie Greloux